Six

Times

Forever

Six Times Forever:

A POETIC RECOLLECTION OF HOPELESS ROMANTICISM

Syed Umar I. Bukhari

First paperback edition April 2019
Cover design by Zarbab Rehman.
Foreword by M.K. McWilliams.

Images 1, 2, 32 by Pixabay
Image 3 by Andrei Lazarev
Image 4 by Xan Griffin
Image 5 by Valentin Antonucci
Image 6 by luizclas
Image 7 by Drigo Diniz
Image 8 by Matt Nelson
Image 9 by Anastasiya Lobanovskaya
Images 10 by Muhammad Nohassi
Image 11 by It's me neosiam
Image 12 by Charlie Hang
Image 13 by Abdiel Ibarra
Image 14 by Bryan Schneider
Image 15 by Marc Sendra Martorell
Image 16 by Sasha Freemind
Image 17 by Joshua Newton
Image 18 by Sean Witzke
Image 19 by Florin Perennes
Image 20 by Stephan Müller
Image 21 by Charry Jin
Image 22 by Maranatha Pizarras
Image 23 by JR Korpa
Image 24 by Vlad Bagacian
Image 25 by Markus Spiske
Image 26 by Tookapic
Image 27 by Ian Espinosa
Image 28 by Elicia Edijanto
Image 29 by Ali Arapoğlu
Image 30 by Rosie Fraser
Image 31 by Samuel Schneider

ISBN: 978-1-7975-3337-7
ASIN: B07P2K5V3H
www.panaceaofrhapsody.wordpress.com

FOR THE DREAMERS,

words can change the world, love.

PRAISE FOR SIX TIME FOREVER

Six Times Forever is a gem. Syed Umar Bukhari combines poetry with prose and dialogue, and the resulting effect is like listening to a great storyteller weave a powerful tale. Love is the theme that shines through all of his poems. Love lost, love gained, love in its essence. He isn't afraid to be vulnerable. He isn't afraid to be honest. Everyone needs to read Six Times Forever.

-Victoria Beth (@victoriabethwrites)

Bukhari's debut collection is one that exudes both talent and passion. He expertly weaves together words of love and magic this are sure to penetrate your hearts as much as it did mine. The style and techniques used to craft every piece perfectly allow all the poetry to weave together to reveal an enchanting storytelling experience. Bukhari is a wonderful craftsman and his debut collection is a must-read, especially for all the lovers out there in the world.

-Jennifer G (@untamedwildpoetry)

Fabled love explored well on both sides of the playing field: eternal hope and memories combined with loss and drifting sorrow. The author explores use of language and words very well, differentiating each poem with ease from the last. I'm particularly fond of the segments where the lovers unite in long form conversation because that's one of my favorite writing styles. Be sure to get yourself a copy!

-Eric Keegan (@blankpagesofmine) Author of **"Strange Cars in the Night"**

TRACK LIST

FOREWORD

I don't quite remember exactly how Syed Umar Bukhari came to be my friend. It began as a mutual respect and support that had always just seemed to be to there. The rest came naturally. True enough, he is indeed supportive, and poets all over the world would attest to that. But it is his talent with words that is most striking.

I remember reading his work long before he spoke of writing a book and being drawn in by the rhythm and romance of it. And when he mentioned potentially writing a chapbook of material, I thought it was an amazing idea. As such happens with writers though, he couldn't hold himself back once he started. What was intended to be a short booklet of twenty or so poems bloomed into this beautiful collection of over one hundred and fifty pages of poetry-art you now hold in your hands. It is more than just poetry or only art.

In Six Times Forever, Umar combines stunning prose with his signature poetry to create an intimate and unique view of love and loss.
He has a way with wording and flow that creates twists and turns in sentences; gorgeous crescendos and full stops that catch you off guard in the best possible way.

His honesty here is important, as this collection is clearly written from the deepest essence of his heart. Join these lovers on their journey and experience Umar's unique perspective of passion, heartache and grief.

-M.K. McWilliams.   (Author of Stereospace)

NOTE

You'll see two fonts used:

This

or

that.

Each of them consistently represents
one specific individual.

Per aspera ad Astra.

through hardships to the stars.

-Lucius Annaeus Seneca:

VEILED GAZE.

I am running late; again.
But what glee today,
one gaze at you,
the world runs in circles, and
I see your fiery rebellious tresses wrestle against your veiled head,
I see the bladed burgundy color of your dupatta,
and I feel a flutter inside: gaudy colors are a statement;
I speed by you before I am at loss.

It has been an eternity of time since,
I see you walk in front of me
still
on your way
to your destination,
same
as mine
and I watch you walk away from me one more time.

You do not notice me— I think.

SYED UMAR BUKHARI

But you are not bounded by a barrier, my unrequited;

it is your stunning vitality and brilliance that ruined me.

Another day of walking behind you,
and I wonder how I always arrived just behind you—

two clocks in sync?

Lub, dub, tick, tock, lub_tick dub_tock;

lub, dub, tick, tock, lub_tick dub_tock.

You are bold, unlike me and it is today you gaze me over with your dark smoky eyes,
filled with an unbearable melancholy, I cannot stand it.

I am
MELT

I

N

G.

The heart flickers and I meet your swarthy eyes no longer than eyes can bear the solar eclipse.

Tomorrow

—

I tell myself

—

will be different.

I will be fearless.

But I am not.

Today is probably the last time I can see you.

I must act now before—

--

SIX TIMES.

Oh, of course it was your infectious laughter!

The sound of exuberance.

I don't think I needed more,

except your bubbly pair of
eyes,

as surely as you know the sun
will
rise tomorrow,
I knew
you were
going to be
someone
I was going to dream about
forever
and
ever;
six times a prayer to all my dreams.

SIX VIRTUES OF YOU.

Rosy lips, ruddy cheeks,
black sea of eyes
that filled with the night.
Lush eyelashes complement the pale delight,
a face crafted with gleaming desire,
despite the slight scar on your slanting nose which sets you higher.
Strawberry honey flowing
in a swirling mess;
glossy waves falling down slender shoulders.
A body made fiercely in heaven,
touched with gold and amber.

R4-D5.

Hello, R4-D5.

he typed, anxiety cornering him.

A few hours later:

I kept waiting for you to talk to me so badly
but like I didn't want to come off desperate...

her fingers turned jelly.

She was gasping for breath
though she was alone,
in her own bedroom.

You always looked so handsome.. that grey sweater..
and your swaying tousled hair
melted me over and burned me out.

Oh! I wanted nothing more..
I tried to.. reach out to your friend... you know?
I wanted to give her a piece of paper for you...
but that didn't go like in the movies, haha.
But.. I should have done more...

his muddy eyes reflected a rusty ruefulness as he finished typing.

Perhaps.

Her face lit up like the morning sun, in a wide-grin, before she pursed her lips.
Haha, she is very protective of me, I guess.
*She never mentioned the paper thing... maybe because we had a tes––
I need to talk to her!*

Do you remember what our English teacher said to me...
that one time about daydreaming?

Yes! How could I ever forget!
What was it he said.. ah...this is the best age to fall in love...
a dangerous combination this tender youth and being fooled by love...

How I wished the heavens it were true.
I kept praying, oh please, let her fall for me...
Like pleading with God... for you.

I wish I had the courage to talk to you earlier, too.
We could have had so much more time...

But maybe we would have been an awkward mess and you would have forgotten

about me

before graduation next month,

he rubbed his eyes.

But what matters is, we crossed that roadblock, you know?

Never!

A burst of nauseating worry overcame her.
She regretted sending it.

Maybe you're right. But we still have time, right?

All of forever,
R4-D5,
only

all

of

it.

DEPTHS OF DIVINE.

I'm falling,
falling
down

d
e
e
p

into the depths

of divine.

Oh, my love,

I am yours to break, yours to hate,
kiss me, bless me, strangle me,
re-shape me, re-create me.
All is for you, but naught
I seek, except the sparkle in your bewitching

eyes.

ALL ROADS LEAD TO YOU?

Your gaze fell upon my face;
you fell for
me;
I did not:
you loved me
but you were not the one.

I ghosted off
in search of my love;
met you,
more scarred than me.

How could you heal me?
how would you love me?
Your mien reeked with self-hatred,
discomfiting me permanen---

I drove away instantly;

another pursuit
of
happiness
undelivered.

You were more handsome than me;
pretty,
but you were no fun:
bland, boring, brimming with honey on the tongue.

I scuttled off
into the shadows
my heart a broken facade of my sorry
visage.

Where was I to find you, my true,
t
r
u
e,

partner?

Where was I to look for the one
in billions of faces?

How much longer before my body limps,
my mind sees the soundness
my thoughts lose their vigo---?

There!

Since I saw you for the first time trailing behind me,
preoccupied, preternaturally precocious in your pretense,
perilous
for hearts like mine---
to when we talked hours on end most days and nights...
you were on my mind all the time.

When you write, I want to read every word.
You smile, I want to frame that moment on my wall.
Don't you understand?
I'm at a crossroads but all roads lead towards you.

Oh, how I'm tied to your existence
forever
and
ever,
darling, darling. Do not
turn me away.
This pumping heart is rusting away
but I know,
you are the only one
maybe I could be your only vice,
my one
to the moon
and
infinity
beyond.

FORBIDDEN FRUIT OF EDEN.

I catch you amidst the slightest of lip bites,

I think you are lost in your own maze, but

I was glancing at heaven, and a part of me wishes
I had never seen you then
---

because I saw what I would live all my life trying to relive.

How cruel: how agonisingly breathtaking.

Perhaps you're my Adam's forbidden fruit,
and hopelessly my desire
for you
burns stronger;
until it is like a fire of infernal rounds,
a flame that turns sin to wounds.

PARCHED FOR YOU.

I drool over your lips, baby, your raspy, beguiling lips:
how juicy that lower, plump lip looks.

God, how I wish to drink a vial of your angelic poison ivy!

How I wish to hold you,

I cannot.

Can I?

Still
—

I

wonder: will my thirst for you ever be quenched then?

Will my boiling fervid proclamations ever be doused?

INTERTWINED TWILIGHT.

I think it's funny we get to have soulmates in this world...
yet most people don't search hard enough
and refute their existence.
Then there are the hopeless romantics.

What's funny about that?

Wait, yeah so what I was trying to say was that those of us who do find theirs
it feels cruel... brutal of God that we don't get them forever, you know?
By forever, I mean, Heaven or Hell, where ever we go,
why can't we be together everywhere, after this world, now; all the time?
He was rubbing his hands together, and taking swift, shallow breaths.

I don't know... you're right, I think. It's like this time here feels
like a short flash: a second. and like an addict, you desire more doses,
regular, permanent: medicine.
Her lips curved in a smirk.
But what if soulmates are reunited after passing through and we just don't know?

That's... very eloquent.
He chuckled.
Maybe... maybe. Who knows indeed? But what I was thinking was
if it's not that, it might be so we value them... soulmates, you know?
Knowing someone is on the same wavelength and sharing that connection...
you simply don't appreciate someone who's always there.

Yeah. We're hollow without that feeling of home.

She traced her breath behind her hand under the light,
searching, reaching.

MY HEART IS YOURS.

I love you.

No, you don't.

Disbelief swept her. How could she consider his words true?

Yes, I do!

No! You cannot be serious!

Yes, but I do! How I love you, I love you!

The clock struck midnight.

*He had pictured this every night for
the last week, yet not one version like this one.*

I don't.. how can I believe you.. that this,
her hands gestured in circles around her.
this is not some prank?

How could someone like him fall for her?

Don't you see the beauty emboldened in my eyes when they're laid onto you?
his murky eyes turned moist.

No. She saw herself. His eyes were a reservoir to all her ugly blemishes
and beaming insecurities.

They made her feel guilty of a crime she was innocent of;
as if she were a thief in the night stealing the tranquil shadows of the night

If you trust me once... I will prove my love...
I will move mountains for you, or die trying,
because your happiness is all that matters!

You really mean this?

Yes, every word.

He was trembling with mirth.

You will
always
be my north pole. Last year, this new year,
the next, forever.

Then as if checking her phone for the umpteenth time,
she glanced away hastily,
putting it back into her purse.

You forgot to
wish me happy new year, isn't that weird?

Silence ensued before she continued.

Happy new year! I wish we get to see hundreds more
together.

Cento anni insieme.
What?
A hundred years together.
I read it in a book and I loved the sentiment.

He scratched his back and then replied in a hushed voice; unable to
come to terms with the botched moment because of his dumbfounded mind;
it would be the end of him, this monumental failure. Everything was supposed to be perfect
-
unable to comprehend.

How could I have forgotten to wish her?

I thought I did, oh, I feel so stupid. I wanted this to be perfect...
and I messed up... I meant to... and now this feels useless but happy new year.

She turned ever so slightly and gazed ahead:
the ocean calm, the night starless and the full moon ghostly.

The serene was unbroken.

But how long will you love me?

I will always love you; from just before the clock strikes 12
on New Year's Eve to after it does on 1st of January every year;
until the sun is fused with earth and life ceases to exist
and all is wrecked and ruined
we are razed and
I will love you;
until heaven itself pours down and
every star
burns
out
and explodes into supernova
and the world shrinks and I will love you:
always,
until all that remains in existence
is my love for you.

Tears welled in her muted eyes, rolled down and pooled.

And I'll always love you, I promise you, my bebé. Forever and ever...
six times forever.

Butterflies buzzed inside his stomach at the cursory bebé.

Six?

One forever is too short a time
—
I want to spend more than forever
—
more than 2...
3...
maybe 6 is enough...
maybe...
because it was the time God created all our Universes in...
so, it is perfect.
I don't want to do life without you.

No, you are perfect!
I can't believe you're all mine now.
I cannot imagine doing life without you, either, oh
how you have blessed me.

DIVIDED WE FALL; UNITED WE STAND?

Marry me.

The salmon color reflected off the shiny Padparadscha.

Marry you?

Her mother thought she had lost her mind.
How long had she known him anyway?
Time would bring her to her senses.
She had already found a more apt guy.
How would she

ever

convince

her

out of it?
How could she explain to her—-
he was the **ONLY BLOB OF COLOUR** on her black canvassed existence.

Yes, I can't see you getting married to another person. I love you and...

...and I love you, too. But you know how hard it is for me since
my mother may never accept you...
if I choose you...
she would think she was too lenient on me and
I broke their trust... you know how parents can be about love,
especially for daughters—*it is a sin*--but I can't live without you, either.
Maybe my father convinces her like he convinced his parents to marry my mother.
I just... I don't know what to do.

Her heart was in her throat; her hands numb and tears welled.

I.. we'll convince them. I earn enough now...
I hail from a good family... maybe good is not the best word, haha...
but like, I mean, everyone respects our family name, you know?
Its rich heritage going back right up to our Prophet, peace be upon him.
I know your father is a convert and has different values...
but since he is not from here, he might support our love...
it is not forbidden to love in our religion, you know.
It is *built* on love and compassion.

Yet... over time, the narrative was shifted by our society to suit their means.
My point being... it's not all gloomy... you know? We could count on him.
Maybe your father will help us. The one time I met him... he was loving and kind...

And I mean... God would not let separate us either... right?
His eyes closed, his hands rose to his eyes and it was if he was fighting back tears.

How I wish my parents were alive to see this.
He continued.

They would have loved you and be so..
so happy to see that ring on you.
I.. I..

I know we'll be happy. You know?
We'll move to any place in the world you want!

She found her hand intermingled into his.

He rubbed her hands gently, before she nodded.

She gave him her left hand; the ring dazzling on her petite hands.

Together. Together, with you by my side, I can do anything... no... no.
We can do anything!

He rested his head on her right shoulder.
They both stared up into the Heavens; praying silently,
chasing dreams in their heads.

I'm so scared.
she mumbled.

I'm really terrified of the uncertainty in our futures.
I mean what is the point of a future without you?

Her voice seemed to fade towards the end.

You.

You are the point of all existence inherently, my beloved.

Listen, if someone were to guarantee your happiness without me in your life,
I'd.. I'd leave right now!
Knowing somewhere in an alternate reality we're together...
forever,
it would keep me goi...

The river in his eyes threatened to flood as he choked up, incapable of coherence.

But.. Nobody could do that and I can't risk leaving you
with someone who might hurt you.

You're too precious.

Don't leave me. Marry me. Grow old with me.
Please, never leave me. Take me in your arms.

With those words she found herself drawing towards him.

And in that embrace, she found eternal peace. A timeless vortex;

an everlasting sense of vigor, and in that moment all was right.

She could die; but it would be a death worth dying for— a life well spent.

STARDUST, DARLING.

Oh, you piece of divine holiness,
blessed to have been made mine for all your wholeness,
how unaware you be, of your immaculate beauty,
no longer are you of just another lot,
no longer does my heart beat out of sync,
it's all coming down, this fall,
it's all coming down, this beautiful, plain, bare night.

You and I, written on the asterism above our heads,
distance a meaningless witch
casting unnecessary doubts inside the magna of our bodies.

Stare above your head, **darling,**

your questions will transcend to dust
and

A

S

H

E

S

---

stardust filled with our promises.

Saiph sparkles a hue of blue,
the darkness witness to the hushed whispers,
your eyes a revelation of the solar eclipse upon us:
our eyes a reflection of the broken souls
rendering inside,
on borrowed time.

The Orion flickers, flickers, flickers,
the world fades
sometimes;
the eclipse of my body on the horizon.

Scarred bodies, crazily in love.
Traumatized heads, madly in love.
Anxious hands, deeply in love.

You are my strength;
wanness,
all that is in between.

Yet all I see is everything
when I stare into your ravenous wormholes
all is lost.

It's coming down this, this fall,
oh darling, it's all coming down.

DOUBT NOT THAT I LOVE.

I am a dove flying through the oceans,
I am a falcon riding the tides of the sky.

I am a slave; forsaken to the pursuit of love,
I am an addict; chasing the high in your fragrance.

I am a lover; strung to your harbor of pearls,
I am a hopeless; wishing you doubt not I love.

Oh but I love ardently, vehemently, intensely,
my beloved. I ask you; I beseech you not to...

It breaks me, ruptures my wretched, forlorn, *lucky* soul:
to have known you, even if it was only ephemeral.

Such, not an apothecary dare cure me without a dose of your luscious lips;
the taste of raspberry.

My heart beats to your name.
My lungs breathe in desire of your grace.
My body aches to meet yours, feel yours.

My lips quaver in worship, imploring God to grant me, my most precious.

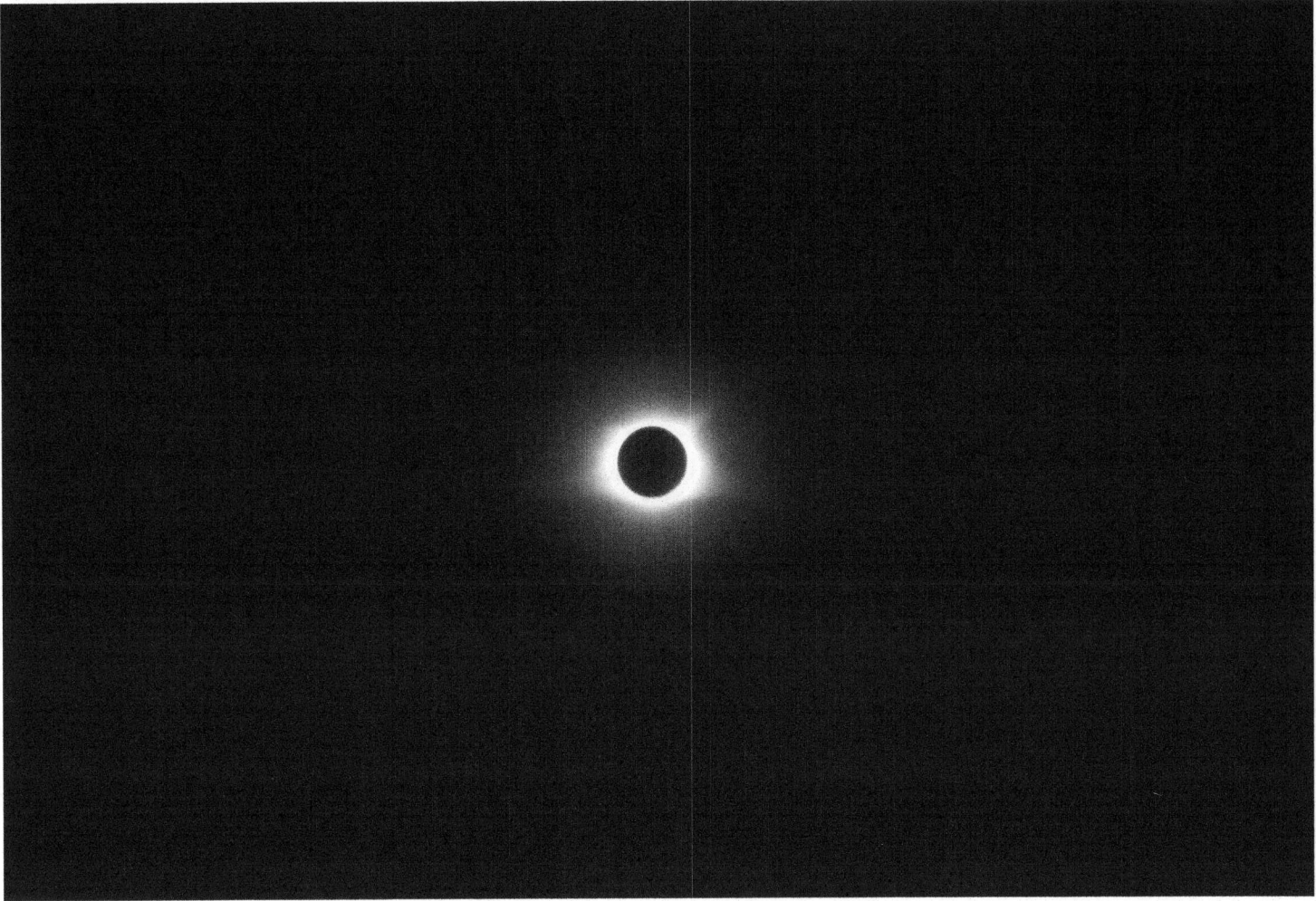

May you doubt the love of the Sun for its Moon, the abundance of stars,
the gleaming of rainbow, the echoing of clouds,
the screaming of cellos, the yearning of poets:

oh, my beloved, do not,

do not,
d
o
u
b
t
my love,

I do love, oh, how I love.

LOVE IS ...

The rustle of the trees, the sputter of the twigs,
my love for you is all there is.

The hunting of loss, the crying of the clouds,
your love for me is bound by no river.

The brittleness of iron, the rust of color,
somebody tells me, soulmates are a lie; marriages run dry?

INTERVAL

I'M SORRY.

Please don't leave.

It required all his strength to utter these words.
The toll of recent times was not lost on either soul.

I don't love you anymore.

Why? You loved me until last night!
his voice cracked;
his gaze searched for warmth;
a candle run out of wax.

Yeah. I just don't feel the same anymore.
I'm really sorry.

Filled with an endless grave of ink,
sorrow and ache,
her obsidian eyes reflected Tartarus in all its abyss and
void.

Bu.. But I can't live without you. I can't even sleep without thinking about us.
His body trembled, his voice turned hoarse, lips quivering.

How is this... How is this so easy for you?
You promised you would never leave! Please... just...

did you ever even love me?

Words did not follow; they need not.
Everything inside him broke. His muscles turned taut;
unaware of tears rolling down his face.

I don't know. I guess I might have. I'm so sorry.

No, please. You promised you would stay forever!
his body ached as he let it wail.

He wanted to get up from this nightmare,
but what do you do when you realise that the nightmare
is your reality?
What do you do when you are with someone you love,
but they're long gone and only a shell remains
--

same appearance,

same body,

same eyes,

same everything

except

heart and soul.

When you lose someone so dear.
When you're only left with freckles and bits of haunting memories.

I love... I love you so much. Please, stay.
I will do anything for you! I am sorry!
Just give me one chance... stay...
I can't live without you... how can you be so... ruth...less?

Oh, naive boy.

She wasn't coming back.
She had
gone

cold.

DAPPLED LIGHT.

Her sooty eyes, lingering
scent of her body and enticing
laughter that shone on.

SHAMED WOULD BE APHRODITE.

Harsh winds of January,
lovely drifts of snow,
the moonstone shines;
euphonious sound of rain clattering your window,
cruel weather sets us adrift, sets us apart.
My lips quaver to God, begging.
I see your midnight eyes, dark and dreamy,
filled with melody, betraying the puffiness,
homes to my silent prayers,
I know not how,
what I owe, how we lured back.
Heavens, ~~my~~ life is a gift, our life,

a moot of nothing(*ness*) on radar,
I hold you, and dip into the deep inside.
Mascara smudged, your beauty sends a quiver down,
my spine, nothing as perfectly arched as yours,
I would worship you, as you are.
Shamed would be Aphrodite,
I am thirsty, my lips wrinkled,
my hunger insatiable, I need,
what my apothecary cannot provide:
a drink from your ocean, off your lips;
to devour your scent; I am yours. You rub my temple,
your delicate hands embrace my ragged face.
A pulse used to flow, now it's a calm,
our heartbeats a mess of rhythm;

familiarity—*stray we had long been*—creeping.
Whispering beside your right ear, I confess
my sins, **darling**, a multitude of my sins;
have I not sinned blasphemy by abandoning you.
Time poured; minutes soared.
Seconds roared in agony, how I swore,
My hair, unkempt and untrimmed, scrape your skin,
your hands explore my neck, running downtown.
You take my lips, lure them inside your mouth,
your divine tongue links mine,
your luscious lips part. *Eureka!*, again;
I moan, pleasure and ecstasy taking control.

Frozen, still,
minutes race by, finally,
you shake your wild, untamed hair, shades of red amber.
The spark in your eyes makes words superfluous;
worry turns to joy, smile lighting up your countenance.

You whisper back, your words pianissimo,

...so much... so much.

I am whole.

HONEY WHISPERINGS.

I'm terrified this won't last:
you don't get to feel whole unless you're going to be broken soon.

Why won't you let me be happy? Why do you want me devastated?
Not again. Not again.

I want to be happy. Whatever cost it. I want to be with him.
I want him like the moon needs your light, Sun.
I want him like a pious man needs to hold onto his faith.
I need him like the oxygen of my breath,
leave us alone,
leave us alone,
leave us alone.

He's all mine. He's all mine, he's mine!
Not again!

L
E
A
V
E.

APPLE HONEY BURNS.

Baby, we walked on wire, wire, wire
waiting to go higher, higher, higher
until our wings were clipped by the gods above us.

Mercilessly mutilated for our mutiny of hearts,
you held me, and locked your eyes onto me,
mine scanned your face adagio.

The velvet-black eyes, the plump cheeks, and
those enchanting lips,
and oh, how you ruined my tongue for anything else!

But to be covered in your scent, in your perfume
my sweet valentine—

Apple honey burns my sallow lips:
even chaos is order yet unlearned.
Ecstatic dazzlement is on your mind
and I realised then:

it's better to be held than holding on.

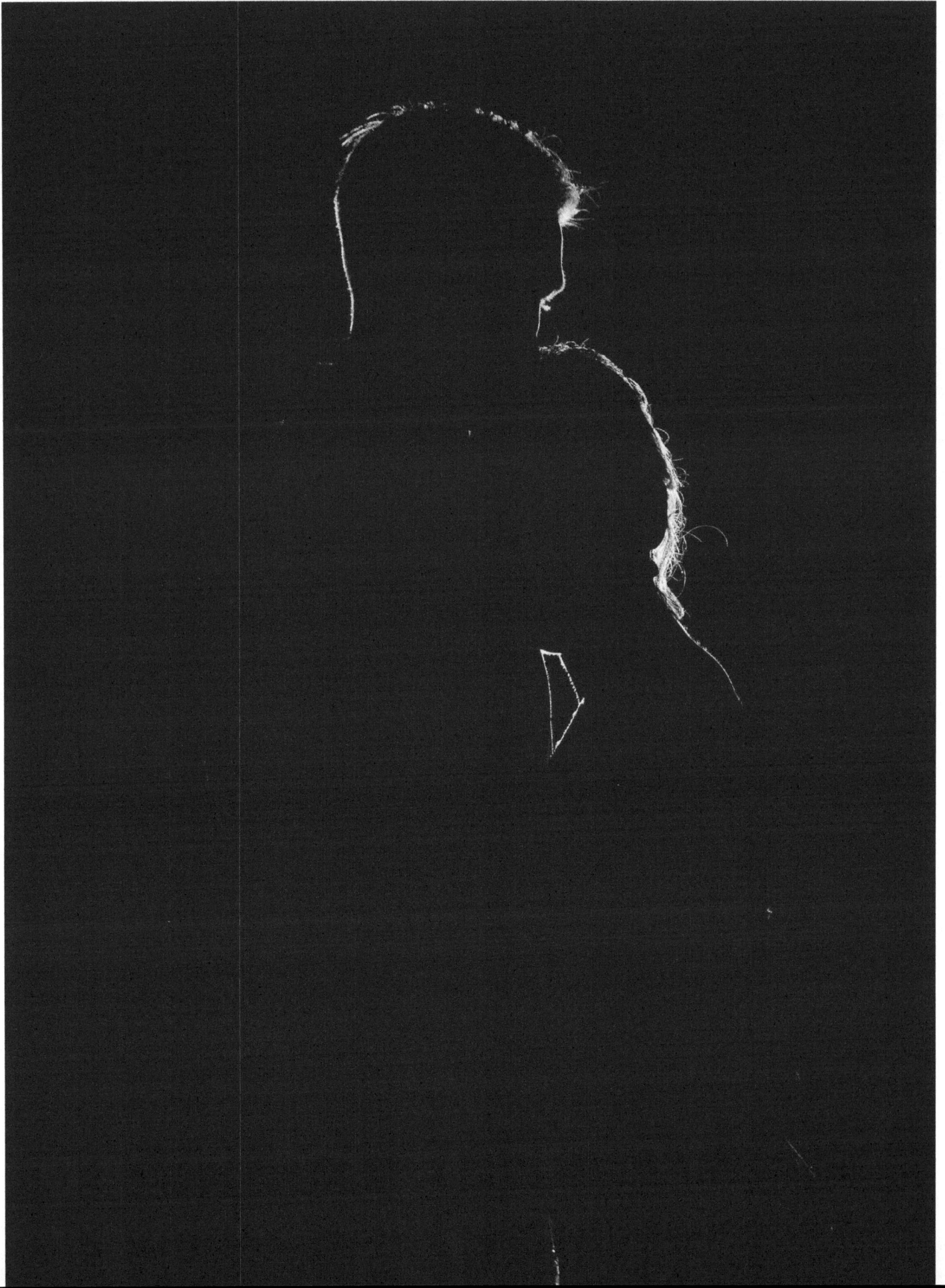

NOCTURNAL ECSTASY.

As we lay together,
moonlight exploring your body,
you run a hand into my thick strawberry-honey hair,
ever so delicately.
I feel a current run down my spine,
and then, you touch my left cheek.
Such a gentle, firm touch
—

slowly tracing the ragged scar on my nose and
tenderly covering it with your lips.

Until you drench me all over,
taking your sweet time;
every inch of my face yearning for yours in a desperate plea of amorous lull
—

I am draped with you.

The absence of your touch for an instant feel like an imprisonment,
double life sentences, oh how long it feels I cannot express
---

eloquence be damned.

You are unrelenting and I want you to be relentless.

I moan, and my body distorts;
I feel goosebumps over my skin;
sensations I never knew existed spill all over my body,
dampening me.

The shadows in the night
sole witnesses
to a symphony of us;
the mellifluous rhythm as we unite,
only to part
and
reunite
again:
in a harmony.
I am in ecstasy.

WITHHELD MERCY.

I'm terrified.
Please, give me the will to do it before I lose the strength to.
I am not ready.
Why did you bring us together?
Why do I deserve this?
No,
Lord,
have

m
e
r
c
y

on this sin-clad person of yours.

I can't hurt him again,
I can't break again;
how could there ever be salvation to wash
me

p
u
r
e
?

THE BURNING (hu)MAN.

You are the brightest part of my existence, you light up
my world
in a glitz, I wish I could be some blazing
Sun
but I am just a man,
a mortal succumbing to the minutiae,
of life that encompasses,
but you, not you, you fight back.

You make your own rules, your own kingdom,
your heart is strong, it beats, beats;
possessed by an animus that transcends the ranks of deities,
you, you, all glory be to you and your Exaltedness:

glory, glory, glory!

Your dainty veneer burns aloud, smoke tunneling into the sky,
the clouds escape away, the stars shine apart, the snowfall greys,
I am in awe, of all your fierce cachet,
I know not how to act, the nerves of my body jarring.

My heart beats, beats, …. … … … … beats… beats, beats.

My heart … … … … thumps, thumps, thumps---

I lose sight of the vision,
wait, is it still

you

I see?

Are you glowing? Why are you walking wit.. are you on fire?

Am I imagining things again?
Is this another sleepless chimera where I see you burning?
I rub my eyes, praying I have answers when I open my gazers,
But confusion befuddles me,
and I am

d

i

s

o

r

i

e

n

t

e

d.

Was it a hallucination, or a waking fantasy?
Gone is the jarring blaze:
—

do I wake or fall again?

Where am I?

Oh, sweet baby, mi amor, how could I watch you set yourself
alight?

Scorching, frazzling, splintering.

No, I'm dead,
I'm dead,
I'm dead.

I slap my head over and over, again, again.

The snow has numbed me, my tongue verklempt,
but you are the one that inspires me,
do you know I would
worship you;
then,
how can I
let you burn?

If anyone were to be apotheosized, it would be you,
Master of my Heart, Sovereign of my Soul;
you are what this world needs,
you are made of the fairies in tales,
you are the goodness that keeps ~~my world~~ our world revolving.
The stardust inside you is incomparable,
it must be tagged, preserved:
I cannot let you burn; I would rather be burned myself!

You are sunshine on this chilly night,
the light that pushes darkness aside,
you are my Himmel.

Not this... figure of flames on a frigid night.

I want to be the begrudging sky,
I want to be the apothecary that would heal you,
I want to be the all-molding clay to prevent any harm on you…
…you must live, you are alive,
you will stand and talk to me;
alive…
won't you?

SYED UMAR BUKHARI

Then why do your black eyes reflect a dark grey-blue of nothing(*ness*)?
Your gaze is vacant, your face crestfallen,
yet a smile curls the corners of your lips upwards and aside;
radiance emits off your face

---

a wholesome smile.

What happened, what, I... I ... did I do this?
No, I'm dead,
no, no, no,
I'm dead:

glory, glory, glory.

You, I would drink all your sorrow,
I would serve you for a lifetime,
you are the hope inside a cave cornered into an abyss,
you are the clap of thunder,
you are worthy of veneration for all your benevolence.
I remember the last time I was under the same roof as your hallowed being,
I was, I was, I was uh-enraged at you, at me, the world.

The last words I uttered to you until now flash me with embarrassment:

Yeah? I wish you're never happy.

So, foolish; so, silly. I pushed you away and then I
waited for you to come back, before
I realised...
I needed you more than you needed me.

Until now, I believed it,
to portray myself as the victim;
no more!
no more!
no more!

70

We needed each other in equal amounts,
the mess we were.
I took that away and now I cannot stop thinking of you,
about you,
for you,
dreaming,
chasing
you.

Love of my life,
please
forgive
me
—

the light flickers, the radiance curtailed,
leaving
the night in complete and utter darkness.

WHY ARE YOU STUBBORN, FATE?

You were my purpose, my will to be,
you were all the good in my life,
but soon were you to leave my side again.

Hapless, hollow and melancholic:
you spoiled my heart, then ruined it for everybody else.

Nowhere to be, nobody to turn to,
neither nary, nor merry,
only to leave it crumbling, in ruins,
I slumped, struggled, and sank,

but fate would not have that, no.

My fortunes were on a surreptitious tide,
unbeknownst to me, I found a confidant,
I found an outlet,
an entity with no judgements bifurcated.
I was lonely, no more, I was terrified, no more.
I could finally smile because I wanted to.
He called me back to the light:
I could finally be
--

but fate would not have that either.

Back was I to being a subdued,
despondent
and
little brought joy,
ennui,
everything passed by.

Feeling eluded my apathetic heart,

and fate would finally have that.

SIX FEET UNDER.

Up all night
the moonlit glow illuminates
me
and obscures my silhouette:
to you I am more.

Twilight, putrid.
Stupid.

Broken, disconsolate.
Aesthetic.

Ruing my life,
I find no meaning to further my inhabitation,
what is left for me
I know of nothing.

Sometimes I lay awake, wondering
if you did not leave, if
we would be us?
Would we still fit the same indentations—
would I have a meaning?

Perhaps when I am
six feet
under
you will miss me.

Maybe not,

no,

definitely

not.

HOW ARE YOU?

How are you?

She asked, softly,
her left hand brushing her upper thorax,
as her gaze fell towards her black pumps.
The salmon of her ring still sparkling on her fingers:
she never took it off.

How am I? HOW AM I? How am I.
You of all people don't get to ask that!
How dare you. How dare you!
You want to ask me how I am,
as if it matters to you.
As if you care. As if you love me.
No.
I will not keep pouring my soul out to you anymore while you undermine my existence.
You don't deserve to know.
You don't deserve to know how you hurt me.
There was a time I wanted you not to let me go. I needed you to hold on.
You never did— not when I cried to you late nights and you brushed it off,
not when you came to me and I actually thought it was because you missed me.
I still grieve.
Of all the means you could wound me with, you chose silence.
The writhing agony.
I will not tell you of my suffering so you can go about your life like nothing.

I will not tell you how you promised me forever,
and ever; six times forever. Then left eons before one.
So, no.
I will tell you nothing. I can't tell you.

But how long will I hold onto this pain?
How long will I pretend to hate you but never hate you?

Ich werde frei sein.
Ich werde frei sein.
I will be free.

I will be free of this toxicity.

Please let me go.

He was staring daggers into a void, down a murky road that led to his salvation.

I forgive you!
It was not your fault. I am not as perfect as I believed.
I'm sorry I held on to this for so long. I'm sorry for everything
but I am leaving tomorrow.
I'm sorry I never realised how hard it must have been for you.
You don't have to hurt anymore. I'm so sorry.

She was at a loss for words, a look of perplexity.

DANCING TO THE RHYTHM.

All of me,
plays as I serenade our gleaming
moments, close
to my heart, crossed,
I cannot look past
you, the grin you would put on
when we went out to feast.
Feast for my eyes,
I say
when the only treat for my
aching
eyes
was the sight of you, sweetheart?

In that moment,
I was forlorn;
In a sumptuous garish, dancing to the rhythm of your body:
imagined.

SET ME ALIGHT.

Time, I thought it would rush
to a stop when
you left me, alone in the
wild unknown,
knowing
I would never survive without you.

You dragged me down,
into this eerie town.

Holding me down,
I believed I would drown.

Surviving the wreck pushing me down,
I realised it was all I would ever surmount.

Hold me down,
I forget our first argument
--it fades--
· what else is out of bounds?

Seconds have cascaded into minutes flooding into hours,
years; hundreds of days and countless moments
—
a forever without you.

My heart
is desperate evermore to steal a glance of you but
nay! My bloodshot eyes find you not,
I am woebegone except in every person I see you:
a tic that reminds me of something you once did;
a feature that reminds me of a moment with you
--
do you still? I wish I knew.

I want to be the reason you laugh,
once again.

I want to be the reason you're caught off-guard
blushing: reading my messages.
I want to be the reason you forget
what date it is tomorrow,
before I surprise you with our anniversary,
only for you to laugh your head off
playing along with me.

Always waiting for you to turn around,
always hoping for your hands in mine,
a ring to shine eternally,
clothes to rainbow fine,
a love that sets us burning alive.

The candles above us flickered, flicker, flickering.
Your eyes reflect the blazing sun of the melted wax.

Miracles, miracles, I want miracles in my life.
The first would be you.
The next would be you.
The last would be us.
Maybe we could still be a symphony of broken hearts;
maybe we could learn to play, learning the concinnity of our bodies.

You, who God crafted out of no ordinary dust.
You, who God must have taken His time on, perfecting your imperfections,
your dust more mabestice than all stardust combined.

The stars out on a stricken night
light up once I mention you.

I catch a few of them ruddy, but they speak no more.

Kiss me on the mouth and set me free, but please don't bite.

I wonder if all our fingers can still trace
our hands, if my eyes still flutter.
If my heart skips a beat or two.
If your skin senses a pulse of electricity
on a touch, just one, **mon chéri**, only one to revive me.

Set me
a
l
i
g
h
t
.

W
O
N
T
Y
O
U
?

Will I see you again, once more?

DESERTED RAILS.

These deserted rails call upon me,
I wish it were autumn and
I heard rustling of trees in places never seen.
Perhaps it snows: I find a heart melting in the fierce cold.

A paradox-: I dream.

I am autumn and winter,
I am a concoction of your figment.
I am a creature of delight.

I quit, I don't want this quiet, it is piercing
a new beginning, climax and ending.

Harsher than the climate, friend to naught but my foe.
I would rebel but my fingers go numb and I cannot
predict when my fingers freeze to the fleck.

The sun shines and I am awake,
I squint around, the unbearable heat feels cold,
or is it my flesh and bones,
the mural of my heart gone mute?

SWEET BECKONING.

Come, come on and join us,
so they say,
but little do you pay attention to
their motives, their masks.
Like a beguiled puppet, you fall,
but soon you find out the sham for its true verity;
deceived and devastated,
you hide in your corner
in the dark room.

Come, come on and join us,
will you stop listening;
will you please not follow;
will you ever learn?

Come, come on and join us,
open your eyes and look,
see them for the truth,
open them wide,
stare into their souls.
Do you see what is there, tucked away behind
the charade of quintessential lies?

Come, come on and join us,
stop listening,
stop listening,
stop listening.

Hear the breeze,
hear the tides,
hear the music of the birds.

Pay no heed to these bogus, make-believe,
the insincere, the hypocrites, the hurtful heap.
Come, come on and join us, dear friend.

A FECKLESS SPECK.

Bad days outweigh,
loneliness coats my skin like paint
all over.

Often, I fail to wash the stains
shadowing me like dark clouds: menacing and harsh.

My existence is hollow.
my mark unremarkable on this world,
so what was it worth?

I dreamt to be yours
I dreamt to love true but
it was only chimerical, love
true as it can be and was for others,

my feckless being is
undeserving: wehe mir!
Woe to all of me.

N
o.

Woe is me.

THE DEVIL POURED SUGAR ON ME.

When I step into the shadow,

it consumes me into the night.

When I step into the light,

it disseminates into the bright sun, cascading away.

When I step into the maelstrom,

I can never quite hear myself; voices
--
ramifications of the
the unquiet cacophony unhinging my synapses

When I step out of my comfort,

my legs are jelly; a gift of solace.

When I step towards You,

I cripple.

When I step away from You,

I get torn to ruins:

I dash for the exit, but I find none.

This is my denouement.

BROKEN WITHOUT YOU: A MESS OF ME.

I can't sleep... maybe I can–

not swing into the sunset,

but I know that, right?

So, what is this... this

mood?

It cocoons me,

warms me,

suffocates me.

I'm cold.

I'm lonely.

I'm freezing.

I wish I were not anxious about holding you in,

I try,
I try,
I try.

I hate myself.
I'm a loser; a freak, an outcast.

Irritable.

Why am I like this?

I can't sleep... maybe I can–

not ride the horizon,

but I know that, right?

So, why do I find myself in...

lasting doldrums, no end in sight.

It blinds me,

it holds me,

it strengthens me.

I'm fragile.

I'm nebulous.

I'm insubstantial.

I wish this nothingness would leave me,

I try,
I try,
I try.

I hate myself.
I'm a loser, a freaking freak— a reject.

Irascible.

Why am I born for this?

I can't sleep... maybe I can—

not walk the landscape,

but I know that, right?

So, why do I find myself wandering...

an aching haze; I was never good enough.

It wakes me,

It comforts me,

It rips me.

I'm frail.

I'm falling.

I'm fallen.

I wish I were better than this.

I try,
I try,
I try.

I hate myself.
I'm a loser, a freaking freak of nature— a reject of society.

Wistful.

Why am I still alive?

THE MAP OF YOU.

The shore is wild, untamed, unfurled, unruly;
so were you.

The morning sun swelters on the barren twines of nature's reed;
sucking up the water, the pumice.
The afternoon sun is steaming, ferocious, effervescent;
so were you.

The scent of you lingers on,
wafting off into the wavering waves of wilting willow where we wrested.
The music in my ears is mysterious in its roots but melodious in its fruits;
so were you.

The strong fight out of chains,
channel their chakra,
check out of the weak post.
The spontaneity, the courage to fight your beats of heart on
in a desire to embellish and live what you feel is life:
the resolute will to bear everything blows dust in the faces
of your doubters
in a blitz.
Glass is strong
--
withstanding high pressures before it crumbles rather than bending
--
a testament of virility;
so were you.

The
railing renders rowing redundant
but brittle bits break
its spirit before the soul singes silently.
Silky smooth, shiny silver,
the iridescent glow of the moonlight is illuminating;
a lavender scented glow,
so were you.

UN ODE À AMOUR PERDU: LA FLEUR SAUVAGE SANS MERCY.

(AN ODE TO LOST LOVE: THE WILDFLOWER WITHOUT MERCY.)

My heart swings atop table tops in a rage of slur.
It spins, round and round the babel of sin.
Nought is won; nought is gain; the heart is vain.
I am alone, thy presence unknown.

'Till it is all I desire in this hour
of madness and fury and fickle lust.
'Tis crowd of faceless masks discomfit:
the rock that cracks is a heart that breaks
--
vulnerable to frights:
I am alone, thy presence unknown.

Fade far away, dissolve and wreck to smithereens.
The darkness: embrace me.
The blue of skies inspires calm but
the sea of storm is unwilling to qualm.
I am alone, thy presence unknown.

The rustling leaves wither and decay,
not unlike the hearts that break:
ruminating reprise.
Let me follow ye, to Heaven or Hell:
thou are my Himmel and I'll follow thee to Hell
because nothing matters except thy love.
All thou ought to know on this earth is a simple truth:
love heals and love hurts but it is my religion; so are you
--
I am alone, thy presence unknown.

Thou were the only one I ever loved:
the only one I will ever love.
Maybe this chill will
freeze all my senses and turn
my heart to stone cold
an herb to cure my ailing heart.
But darling, I love thou so ferociously

I hate thou because I love thou to the extent of physical ache,
and
I am alone, thy presence unknown.

If I could, I would paint havoc over everything,
for eternity pushed us away.
If I could, I would torment the storms,
unleashing a torrent of rampage amidst
the rains of stupor that fool thee into somnolence and
how can I pass into nothingness when I loved thee with all of my heart?
Unearthly in your grace, bedazzling in thy motion, and
I am alone, thy presence unknown.

We learn from an early age a beating heart is cause for joy.
How else dost thou keep with this incessant game of charades?
What a weapon to hold in a war that will be
the end of us, the end of us, the end of us,
the end of all.

Except thy bliss, that will see no end in its multitudinous bounty:
I want to hear the melodies of thee:
I want to hear the tunes of thy lips orchestrating the sonnet of thy body;
unheard of: I want to slice at my taut addiction of thou dripping berry;
oh, how all of me is thine:
then
am I alone, thy presence unknown?

Please end my guise, please take me away, far from the tease of thou.
I want to come home now, home to thee, home away from mine, end this pursuit.
Hold me, hold me onto thee, cling to me.
Haunt me, heal me; hallow thee.
I have seen perfection before; a rainbow in the skies; a Beethoven symphony;
how insignificant compared to thou sight
in a moment of ecstasy; the euphoria a lyre to fancy;
but am I alone?

Thy presence unknown.

A BALLAD OF (CONTEMPORARY) MELANCHOLY.

My heart swings over table tops in a rage of slur.
It spins, round and round the babel of sin.
No victory; no gain; the heart is vain.
I am alone, your presence unknown.

Until it is all I desire in this hour
of madness and delight; fickle lust.
This crowd of faceless masks disengage:
the rock that cracks is a heart that was broken

--

undeserving of forgiveness:
I am alone, your presence unknown.

Fade far away, disseminate and wreck to smithereens.
The darkness embraces me.
The blue of skies instills calm but
the sea of storm is unwilling to qualm.
I am alone, your presence unknown.

The rustling leaves wither and rot,
not unlike the hearts that break/
paranoid android.

Let me follow you, to Heaven or Hell:
you are my Himmel and I'll follow you to Hell
because nothing matters except your love.
All you need to know is a simple truth:
love heals and love hurts but it is the joy of our lives
--
I am alone, your presence unknown.

You were the only one I ever loved.

You:
the only one I will love.
Maybe this chill will
freeze all my senses and turn
my heart to stone cold
skating through ice and frozen soul,
a pill to cure my ailing heart.

But darling, I love you so ferociously

I hate you that I love you,
and
I am alone, your presence unknown.

If I could, I would pour havoc over everything,
for eternity pushed us away from us.
If I could, I would torment the storms,
unleashing a torrent of rampage amidst
the rains of stupor fooling you into somnolence and
how can I pass into nothingness when I loved you with all of my heart?
Breath-taking in your grace, bedazzling in your motion, and
I am alone, your presence unknown.

We learn from an early age a lying heart is true;
how else do we keep up with the incessant game of charades?
What a lethal weapon to hold in a war that will be
the end of us/
the end of us/
the end of us/
the end of all.
Except your bliss, that will see no end in its multitudinous bounty:
I want to hear the melodies of your tune:
I want to hear the rhapsodies of your lips resonating your body;
unheard of: I want to slice at my tense addiction of you, oh, you:
then
am I alone, your presence unknown?

Please end my guise, take me away, far from the tease of you.
I want to come home now,
home to you,
home away from mine,
end this undying pursuit.
Hold me,
hold me onto you,
cling to me.
Haunt me,
heal me;
hallow you.
I have seen perfection before in a rainbow in the skies/
a Swift concert/
the feeling of diving from the sky/
how it pales to the feeling of exuberance; the euphoria
I feel on the sight of you.
But I am alone.
--
(of course!)
--
your presence unknown.

SAD, BEAUTIFUL, TRAGIC.

I reek of failure;
why am I breathing? Death please
take me in your arms.

Drown me.

Don't

m
o
u
r
n

me.

THE BIRTHDAY SONG.

You stand around, rubbing your hands with anxiety,
you are excited and ambivalent, and you don't like uncertainty,
you tell yourself it will be okay, you occupy yourself.

The clock ticks on,
the clock ticks on,
the clock ticks on.

You sneak a glance every minute or so,
any time now!
Surely,
any time now,
midnight will eclipse,
and it will be:
happy birthday, happy birthday to you.

You're a fool for being excited,
you're a fool for thinking anyone will care,
you're mistaken in thinking someone's going to be preparing
for this moment
for months,
you're utterly crazy if you imagine words being written
for you.
You're foolish if you think this day should matter, why?

The hours pass by,
you feel dejected.
But you tell yourself to calm down,
take it easy,
it's not over yet
you whisper over and over.

You want to be surprised
---
blown away.

You want to feel like the Centre of the Universe
the way you would do;
you wish she'd come out of somewhere,
a grin on her face;
a chimera come to life,
but you know
-

YOU KNOW!
-

she will not,
she probably does not even
remember.

Happy birthday, then, happy birthday to you!

You want to sob, sob like you never have,
you have probably never felt so lonely or forsaken,
you have probably never felt so unloved,
you have probably never felt such weakness,
you have probably never consumed affliction like you just did,
you want to catharise;
of course, today, even tears betray you, not unlike everyone else.

You make decisions in your head,
you thought you had grown wiser,
but you reproach yourself on that,
long time to that, you think,
eons of catastrophe to persevere before.

You make promises to yourself, vows,

happy birthday then, on this day,
happy birthday,
my friend.

You have grown sick of it all,
you have grown weary,
you were not unafraid of death
now sometimes you catch yourself wondering how soothing
it would be to
just
let
go.
You find yourself imagining the end to this misery.
Sure, hellfire awaits: could it be any worse than now?

You find yourself searching for answers
--
are we alive
before we succumb to fate;
taste death in its finality?

Do we breathe
before an *ax* marks the spot
and we suffocate to obscurity in a sepulcher?

Maybe now when you near death itself,
you finally grasp its grave solemnness,
and you finally fear the next chapter
and find yourself humbled to its imminence?

Maybe.

You are not ungrateful,
you are not suicidal,
you are only tired,
you are just jaded.

Funny thing,
you chuckle to yourself,
being lethargic with all your life in front of you.

But what is all your life you wonder,
what if there is no tomorrow, you wonder?

You see your life as a portal to death:
has it been a meaningful stay then?
Has it been a purpose fulfilled?

You are not unemotional,
you are not worthless,
you used to feel oh so vehemently,
you used to be buoyant with passion for many a thing,
you used to feel a kaleidoscope of sensations
--
a medley of emotions.

You used to feel as sure as the Sun that rises every morning:
you were a good man.
You were one to remember.
You were a good man,
you were
my friend.

Happy birthday,

happy birthday to you.

BEAUTIFUL SAN(E)ITY.

Light seeps away, beautiful sanity.

Pushing my brain into a dazzle of pain,

aching the joints of my bones.

I pierce my razor nails through my veneer,

the tongue flaps out, a shriek escapes.

Blood and butter, bitter bile chokes my desire.

What felt like oblivion only moments ago is gone,

the everlasting interlude waits for no one.

Darkness creeps in, detestable heathen,

leaving me gasping in beaming daylight,

breathless and in bedlam—

I mark the earth under my feet, slipping; sinking; crawling

before I hit the rocks and fade into the black,

singing a saccharine lullaby, here I lie, numb.

What felt like music only moments ago is gone,

the everlasting interlude waits for no one.

THE UNIVERSE (in)COMPLETE.

It started with me,
before you came along to make it two.
The world changed,
it morphed.

You and I became us and two of us the universe.

A happy abode, a fulfilling life.
Two of us,
the universe complete.

But you were imprudent and angsty,
I was grizzled and obstinate.
The two of us,
the universe complete.

I pushed the two into a stupor,
wreaking havoc on all.
I was a fool,
I was reckless despite my years.

You slit your wrists,
the blood pooling around your pair of arms.

I stood there, imagining the two of us,
the universe complete.

Watching and echoing you, staring;
before

my vision greyed into oblivion and the last sig--------

DARKNESS: UNRAVEL ME.

Where did you go?
You were here just now before you vanished into thin air.
I looked everywhere for you, rummaged every nook.

Why are you looking at me like that?
What's with your eyes?
Fish-eye wide? Huh?
Tell me! Talk!

Oh. I get it. Dumb me taking so long.
I'm the crazy one. Yes, you're right!
I have been crazy from the day I laid my eyes upon her,
compelled, fixated and
--
I know what you're doing! I have you figured out now, heathen!
I know what you're trying to do.
You're one of them. I know it!
I'm such a fool. I fell for you. I fell for
you!
Shame be on me! Shame be on me.
You're one of them.

Why? Why would you?
Betray me, like that?
I gave you all of me... was that not enough for you?

Wait... wait. It was never about me... was it?

STOP! What are you doing? NO!
GET AWAY! NO!
I'll... You're.
DON'T!

INTERLUDE

I WISH—

I wish to never be sober again when I'm drunk on you.
I wish I were by your side wherever you are.
I wish this worthless little note is enough for you.
I wish, oh heavens, how I wish.

I wish to be seen.
I wish you would see me.

I wish we still talked.
I wish I were not lonely.

I was I had more to say.
I wish I did not run out of words.
I wish you never left me.
I wish you missed me.

I wish I die soon.
I wish I were a better human.
I wish you forget me.

I wish someone showered me with love.
I wish I were someone's choice.
I wish someone chose me every single time over everything else.

I wish to know
miracles,
miracles,
miracles.

I wish you
—

BEYOND THE WONDERLAND.

Heart craves what eludes,
irrational thoughts cloud my judgement,
leaving me parched for the deadly,
dangerous feeling
—
I walk deeper,
into the wonderland.

I am drunk on it.
I am drunk on it,
I am drunk on you,

and I wish never be sober again:
I want you every day, every hour in doses that stun all common senses.

My love, my sweetheart,
my heart's desire.

Why, pray tell, I yearn for you,
still,
as fresh as the wounds never closed,

As my heart beats for the God above us in His exalted-ness,
why am I put to this chase?

What did I do, what do I do?

ALIVE?

My eyes search for
you.

I hear you,

I feel you,

I sense you,

I know it.
Your scent lingers around me all the time, once again.
I know it is you,

whence
you
are still

a
l
i
v
e,

are you
not?

BURN THE WITCH (ALIVE).

Eons ago, lived a witch.

Benevolent, kind, powerful.

Humans hunt, witches die.

Her daughter immolated,

in the middle of the night.

Immolated,

bereaved,

perforated.

Eons ago, lived a witch.

Malevolent, cruel, mighty.

Humans hunt, witches kill.

Her rage burned cities,

in the middle of the night.

Seared,

avenged,

haunted.

Eons ago, lived a witch.

Truculent, mean, merciless.

Humans run, witches feast.

Transfused into a pigeon,

enticing Selene cocooned inside spider flesh.

Prolonged,

sustained,

metamorphosed.

Eons ago, lived a witch.

Silent, fuming, pitiless.

Humans embrace, witches die.

The pigeon plumages,

Selene transmutes into a Rose.

Merged,

reformed,

ruined.

Eons ago, lived a witch.

Virulent, raging, loveless.

Humans distract, witches crowd.

The witch in her true sound,

Rose turns Leviathan.

Maimed,

reigned,

waned.

Eons ago, lived a witch.

Breathtaking, shrewd, broken;

The daughter atoned for sins she never committed; witches rejoice.

The witch in her element,

the daughter survives.

Jaded.

Bruised.

Severed.

Was my mother that daughter?

Is that why she gave me everything and never just forgotten lore?

Is that why I secretly watched her cry tears of rose and lavender?

Is that why I caught her once with raw meat in her hands, blood pouring from her lips?

Her body aged so little; her heart so full.

Too late, too late now, mother.

I'm coming home to you, all truths bared.

THROUGH THE EYES OF A FRAGILE CHILD.

I'm not reliable, I think.

My head blanks and blames

monsters that do not exist; a demon lives

but he is inside me, not my head.

I am fragile, fickle, frail, and

I wish you were mine.

I quickly scribble it down before I forget again.

But who are you that I speak of?

I found a letter from you.

It read:

I am sorry, I love you. I wish I could have...

I do not know what it means except you love me. An instinct.

Did I love you, too?

A reminder of my soul drained down the ravine,
I wish I remembered.

How long did we know each other; was it long
enough to plan a future together?
I must have forsaken you.
A fault from my conception----
Judas holds nothing on me.
I wish I knew what this text on the back of my palm meant.
It is a name, isn't it? It's a letter, I think.
Yours, could it be?
Under my pillow:

What am I looking for?
Why are you listening to me?
Why are you gawking at me?

Who are you?

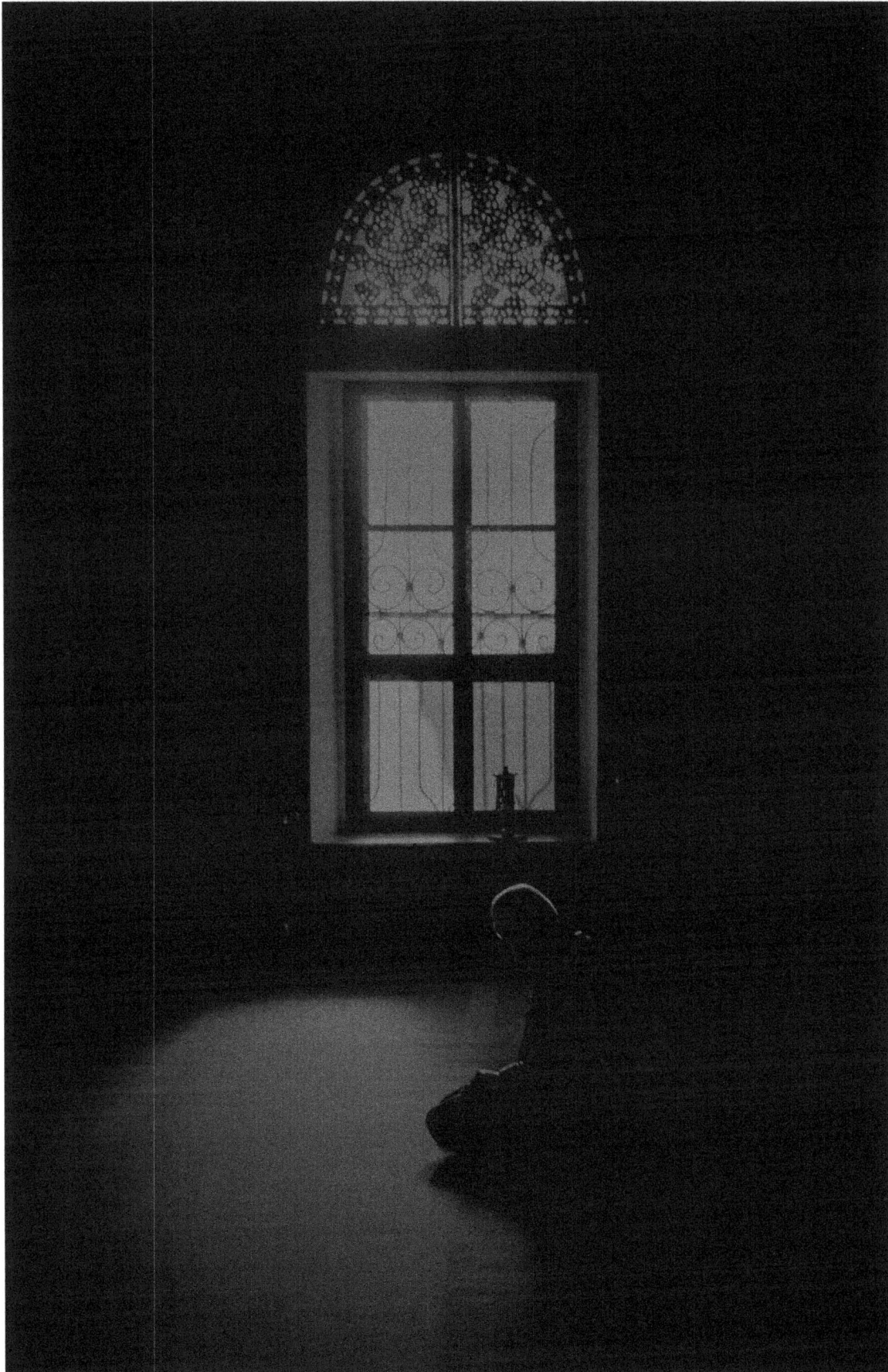

BURIED LETTER TO X.

DEAR X,

Are you doing well? I hope you are doing okay.
I am trying. I try every day.
I think it is expected of me to not write to you anymore,
after all, what are we anymore?
I am told to move on. Move on, heh.

Remember the way we used to know each other fiercely a long time ago?
Best friends? Lovers? Insatiably inseparable?
To
strangers.

I did realise a little after you so recklessly
abandoned me
that I never knew you the way
I thought.

I was bitter for a considerable time,
melancholic, furious, depressed: vehemently.

However, time does heal all wounds,
and mine filled in as a new covering layered itself
upon the older and rotten layer.

My skin was reborn and, in a way, maybe I was too. Maybe.

All that progress and yet the moments I miss you,
oh, totally ruin all bits of progress.
I'm that young, sensitive boy again
— —
intensely in love with you and all of you and just you and only you.
Nothing else matters then. Nothing else exists.

I know you do not care anymore.
Why would you, for someone who never meant much?
Maybe I still care, the fool I am or why would I write this?

I miss you.
I do not want you to know... do I?

Sometimes I catch myself wishing you befall a void,
a black, overshadowing pit,
and you grasp what you did to me one day.
No sooner than I scold myself for such an iniquitous and abominable thought.

Am I a terrible person for that?

I don't know.

But I loved you.
I did love you more than I loved anyone, more than I will.
I have never loved since.
You ruined me; my tongue, my body, my soul: all of me.

I have everything I want, in this moment and
I am grateful for it.
I do not wish... at least you don't haunt
me
in every face
I see anymore. It's a blessing.

No, I'm sorry. I can't finish this. I cannot lie anymore.
This masquerade... I cannot continue pretending I am okay without you:
I miss you. I still love you. I still wait every single day.
I still search for you in every face, wandering like a lost gypsy.

I don't know if I ever told you how I explained your role in my life:
a clot for ailing hemophiliacs;
compelled to you like a sunflower bent to the will of the Light Star;
without you I withered and would cease to be whole.

Cease to be
I.
Annihilated.

I am too late.

NOT YOURS ANYMORE ALWAYS YOURS,
SIGNED.

COME BACK, MY LOVE... MY LOVE?

Gathered today,

we wish you peace and tranquility

and offerings and prayers,

the sound of the impending drop escaped none of us.

Indeed, some of us will be troubled for weeks or months,

scarred today, cursed to carry on.

I look around

rows filled with the corporeal surround me

but what good is anyone other than you?

A pungent strike on my wounds.

I want

to be with you, where are you?

come back, my love, my love?
my love,

I
n
e
e
d
y
o
u.

Accusing eyes meet mine,

as if, as if...

as if I was the one?!

I want to yell in their faces,

claw the façade off.

I am dressed for a funeral,

mine.

I wear black to express the dark inside me,

white to embed you, you were all my colors,

the rain, rainbow, and donuts.

My Heart demands an end,

this melancholia

of my Soul.

I know it will end, blame me not for desiring swiftness,

then, staring at you for the last time,

pallid-faced,

eyes shut and seemingly at calm;

paralyzed.

Betrayed by my tears,

a wise man came to me, remember the good times, he said.

A long

pause

followed.

The stillness consuming me.

Think if he were to be in your place, what would you want?

To let go and forgive?

Perhaps to let go, but never forget you...

to remember;

and I saw you.

A sallow complexion,

your eyes carrying an ache,

a weak smile twitched on your face,

go on,
you said.

WENN DIE NACHT VOLL IST.

(WHEN THE NIGHT IS FULL.)

When the night opens in
trailing plight.
The Haven of wan moonlight.
When the echoes of the Night
scream at my soul, scrounging at the delicate
flesh harkened by the green blues of Time–.
The Woods are a flute, stars scanty;
the gnarly oak trees bare and rot.
Putrid, detestable whiff—
A stupor comes over me.
A sea of haze swarms me into the eerie—
When my heart drops in my colon,
a scaffold of my crime.
The realm of the catacombs of Time.
Invite me to the Black Forest,
host to all unborn:
dead or puff—
Which is the passageway to august Purgatory,
steaming sprinkle of sorrow–.
Close your eyes to the travesty;
footsteps grunge me from above the morass.
The Starlight is pale, vapid—
A contouring shadow of the Full Night.

GREYED RAINBOWS.

Perhaps the sunlight out there
greyed the light in me.
Perhaps the spring out there
blossomed repugnant, repellant flowers in me.
Perhaps the fall out there
bore in me the darkness-borne night of the funeral.

Where am I headed? I search around me.
Whom do I belong to? I search for you.
I was cross, all was lost.
It was the moon; it stole my tune.

Smothering me, no longer is
my existence but
a gaudy
headlight
fuzzes my vision
sometimes.

I find myself inhaling deep breaths.
A lump often finds its way;
maybe I would resist,
if only,
there was something to hold onto.

When we sailed adrift? I wish I could undo.
When we were together? All was rhapsody: we were euphony.
My rainbow awaits me; radiant, smelling like petrichor; elated.

The other side beckons for me.
The lit rooms blind me.
Perhaps I will reconsid
—
I float away. I am a nightingale:
my song serenades You in a mellifluous crescendo of the night before the colors grow insipid.

When was I gone? All I remembered was You, trembling lips.
Forgive my sins, I said, before You take me away.

A sea of obscurity and vile murk
encompassing and embracing in me.

UNSAID; (un)WED; (un)DEAD.

Here he comes from the depths of fire,
my knight in sweltering hell,
amidst chaos and din, clamor and sin, love and war,
the only genuine goodness guarding the lure.

I wish I could have said this to him when he was here,
over
and
over
until he would
never
forget.

I could never tell him why I abandoned him,
why I turned my back on him and
offered nothing in return,
how I ached for his voice, his touch,
he will never know

—

I was not strong enough to hold my heart back from gravitating
out of orbit
when he was nearby.

How would I tell him of the sleepless
nights
I spent when he would text me late night?
Or call me a dozen times and I would

—

could not reply. How would I
tell him of all the times
I could not meet his gaze if I ever stumbled across him.
How I never could look him into his melancholic eyes and be sane!

How could I break his heart over and over and over and over and over?
Even I could not be so cruel.
How would I tell him how I wished I could talk to his mother
and
tell her how sorry I was, how I messed up?
How would I tell him of all the times I spent staring at his photos
and his words,
like a bystander hiding behind a cloth of disguise,
--
furtively proud
of all his accomplishments as he jumped across hurdles
--
visibly unmoved?

How relieved was I when he moved to another country, far, far away?
He will never know. He can never read this, never know.
How relieved not to have to wake up every day knowing I could see him
that day and have my resolve go to zilch.

All the nights and moons spent together,
how could I ever forget that first under a full moon?
The night that made us; the night made us before
the wretched daylight tore us apart.

Only to reunite us that chilly January night.

Oh! How my heart desperately mortars my chest
to tear through the flesh and fascia at the sight of him,
to embrace him,
the absence of him creating a depression in my soul;

my eyes reflections of the hollow.

My mettle cracking open in a gush at the homely sight of him.
My long, long vigil coming to an abrupt end. Before I knew what was happening,
we were inseparable, and I laughing like a fool; uncontrollable;
in mirth. Everything seemed perfect. The moon phasing out and back,
and sometimes I would catch her stealing a glance at us on nights;

envy all over her face inconspicuously; set fixed at him.

Maybe he believes it was easy for me
—
how could I blame him?

Maybe he blames me for ruining us
—
how could I refute him?

Maybe he refutes I loved him
—
how could I deny him?

Maybe... he denies my existence in his life
—
how could I ever defy him?

When he said he forgave me, I swear I thought I was hallucinating!
But then he said it again
and I was sure I could not have imagined it
—
the smile he had on, oh.

I never deserved his forgiveness. I was not
—

I am not worthy. But I try.

I try to be someone I am proud of; I strive to be good.
I can never explain why I did it.
But I needed to do it for myself,
a poor attempt at retrieving some part of my wandering;
lost soul.

These words are worthless now,
except maybe self-assurance that I am not utterly despicable?

I want to scream, wail in his face, in mine; pull my hair out:
Lord, what have I done?

Why had I been such a fool to think separating us would propel him to the skies,
help him see he deserved more than I;
oh, the pain I caused him. How can I forgive myself?
How can anyone forgive me?

I am so sorry, I did not mean to be so cruel,
I did not mean to fall in love with you.

I did not mean to leave you and all the things we had behind,
like paper put to incinerate. I can't
deal with things being favorable,
I can never accept something pure for myself:
I run away.
I run away.
I
r
u
n
a
w
a
y.

When I should have stayed.
I can never forget you, your birthday, our anniversary, our days, our nights.
How could I?
I shouldn't have left you hanging behind.
I know what you must find yourself thinking:
if I would come surprise you someday.
I wish I could. I wish I would not disappoint you over
and

over

again.

It has taken me a forever to be brave enough; a forever we have been apart
and why does the earth keep revolving around
—

how dare it!
—

the sun or the moon the earth...
like nothing went wrong?

I wish it would all stop,
I wish the music turned mute,
the light flickers went out, the fire turned soft; the moon drowned.

How I desperately wish I was still yours and you mine,
oh, this heart still beats for you.
You are the
love of my life,
but it's too late now, my sunshine.
I broke you and I broke myself and I deserve no mercy for my sins;
no atonement; no salvations.

I wish I never did any of the terrible things I did.
I wish I never pushed you away. I wish I were not alive but maybe,
this is my sentence.
But someone will love, someone will love you,
I know someone will love you; better than I ever could.

I wish sometimes that you forgot me; it would be easier on you.
I wish I were not as lonely as I always am.
I wish I died alone, and you never saw me again; you have suffered enough.

Why do I wish forgiveness from you now, God?

Why am I drawn towards you at this hour of dark?

Why do I feel worthy of forgiveness now, my mistakes atoned?

Oh, if only I could do it all over...
oh heavens, I'd never leave you again, **my beloved**,

not once in a forever, never.

Maybe, we'd have our happy ending, maybe our story would not be left incomplete.

Maybe we'd be together,

like we dreamed...

and promised

--
those three words
 we said too much
but never enough.

Six times forever.

I am sorry.

I love you.

ACKNOWLEDGEMENTS

I'm grateful to Allah for helping me find a voice, somehow;

and for the words that flow. I couldn't do a single thing without His mercy or blessing.

It is by God's help that I found the will to complete a book I'm in love with.

I want to thank my parents for always believing in me and pushing me to fulfill my dreams.

I want to thank my siblings for their love.

I want to thank my friends and family for their support

It wouldn't be possible without any of you rooting for me!

Thank you, Zarbab, for the cover design (@zartbab).

Thank you to everyone who supported me on this journey and everyone who supports me.

Thank you to my readers; I am grateful to you beyond words.

LIGHT YEARS APART UNDER THE STARS; FOREVER INTACT?

Cast away, in your embrace,
unscathed vials
of grandeur, magnanimity.

You embraced
me,
fueling
a glimpse of
the bizarre swirl.
Round and round,

f
o
r
e
v
e
r
a
n
d
e
v
e
r.

I hold onto the falling, untamed air,
trying

to grab hold of my ground.

Failing,

               fainting.

     FA

         L

         L

          I

           N

        G.

I meet the gate-keepers roadside,
a blockade
of somber guardians.
I slump
down,
downtrodden.

You show up, above in your high donjon,
strawberry-blonde hair swaying, charcoal eyes seducing,
succulent red lips in a *pout-turn-laughter,*
your body silhouetting against the blinding light.

You walk towards me, shaking your head
before you erupt into a cackling laugh.

But my gaze falls to your beguiling wine chiffon maxi,
and a gasp escapes.

Were we always destined like Zuleika and Yusuf to meet, to diverge?
Reunite? But our tale had a twist, didn't it? Departed yet again.
And what now?

My thoughts scramble,
and I forget everything
----
how did you settle in here before me?
how long had you been here?
how God set us to meet again
----
except our promise
—
six times forever; embedded.

Yo... you actually look better than when I fell for you, ha.

I have so much to tell you I feel my heart will explode, whoosh.

Are you going to keep staring like that or are you going to come along?
Let's not run out the hourglass this time...a forever still awaits. All of it.

Your mouth mimicked the sound,

as your hands acted it out
before you started waving wildly at me,

jigging.

There goes a forever, pfft.

Your hands undulate:

a wave superseding.

Oh, this silence is killing me. Would you talk to me, my darling?

The loud echoes nonplussed me,

before it dawned on me:

what a beautiful way to enter purgatory!

ABOUT THE AUTHOR

Who am I?

I'm more than a skin, more than a name, more than a stupid identity.

I'm more than a body, more than a face, more than a stupid clarity.

I'm an anachronistic soul, a wandering heart; a kaleidoscopic mind.

I'm a writer/poet, hapless and hopeless, a romantic and realist.

I'm a lover of semantics; a predator of banters; a dreamer of wonders.

You can find and follow me on most social media websites (Instagram, Tumblr, Pinterest, Facebook etc.) to stay updated for the latest content.
You can also visit my blog for more poems, writings, ramblings and everything else related to writing or poetry.

ABOUT THE BOOK

The realisation of poetic storytelling and a stunning debut for a melodious poet, Six Times Forever is filled with vivid imagery and hopeless romance. Unique poetry styles complemented by several distinct voices intersperse the book with sprinkles of German limning a visual narrative resembling a medley of exotic stardust.

A tale of two passionate lovers: fervent and fanatic, sizzling and sensuous. Part of the Muslim world where love is still considered taboo, ameliorated with the modern times; surreal in parts; supernatural in others but invariably heart-wrenching and effervescent, like honey draping the heavens.

A tale of obsession and consuming mania; spiraling into madness until it sings as sweetly as a symphony.

A tale of loss and grief: undone; unwoven; unloved?

Six Times Forever.

SYED UMAR BUKHARI

THE END.

SYED UMAR BUKHARI

184

Made in the USA
Middletown, DE
03 May 2019